Beep Beep !

Music That Moves You

by

Chaia May

Cover and interior design by Chaia May and Associates Book Services.

First Published Edition 2016

Library of Congress Cataloging-in-Publication Data

May, Chaia M.

"Imagine Series" - Fun with 3D Shapes
by Chaia M. May

 p. cm.

ISBN 978-0-9864121-3-4

LearningPlay
PUBLICATIONS

Introduction to Beep Beep! Music that Moves Us

How better to get children's attention than with the sound of a train, car or another vehicle? Tying these familiar images and sounds to musical notations connects children to musical language in a lively way.

Learning the meanings of the notations and linking them to cars, trucks and trains helps with recall. This way, the children can recognize the musical symbols after only one reading by associating each one with the colorful, beloved objects. Their learning is further reinforced when they color each object left blank.

I have learned from my students and my own teachers that young children are able to learn what older ones can, only more slowly. They are naturally curious; it is just a matter of how the material is presented that determines whether it will stick or not. We have made the visuals and notations simple and clear. The additional story at the end, with its images, street map and separate, printable pieces offers an interactive method for making repetition fun. Children have literally rushed into my class with a big smile, saying "Chugga Chugga" to show me what they remembered from last week.

I hope you will take this book, sit with your child or classroom of children and run with it as well. You can read the book straight through or reinforce the concepts by repeating pages to create new patterns. You can also use this book as a support for the laminated flash cards of the same content that we also make available.

Enjoy not only seeing the children's music skills grow, but their math skills as well. A whole, a half, a quarter, and an eighth represented in notation are the beginning of recognizing and mastering fractions.

Additionally, this book should prepare your students as it has mine to go right into playing an instrument. With this symbolic knowledge and visceral timing, their focus can be on learning technique. They will already understand and be able to replicate fast and slow tempos, nuances of loud and soft, as well as grasp the direction and order of how the notes are organized in space.

Lastly, I hope you and the children will add melody to the rhythms we present and create your own wonderful compositions. Beep Beep!—using vehicle sounds in step with musical notes and phrases, is only the beginning of the road to loving music.

Warmly,
Chaia

VISIT US ONLINE

Find us at LearningPlay.org. Look under "Publications" for this book and the others in the "Imagine It! Series" where children learn through play.

See my LearningPlay Facebook page too! Please feel free to comment and offer suggestions to the existing material as well as ideas you would like to see in the future for you and your children!

beep beep

honk

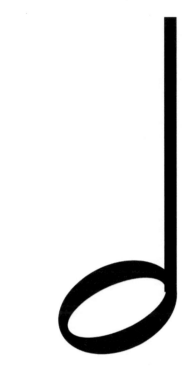

WEEooo

1-2

easy-coloring-pages.com

O

SSSShhhhhsssss

1—2—3—4

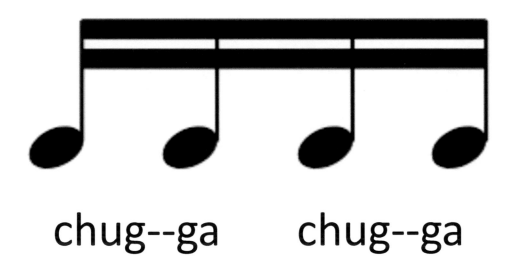

chugga chugga

stop

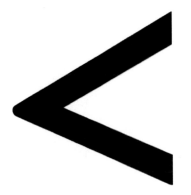

bang

beep-
beep

honk

beep-
beep

honk

chug-ga

chug-ga

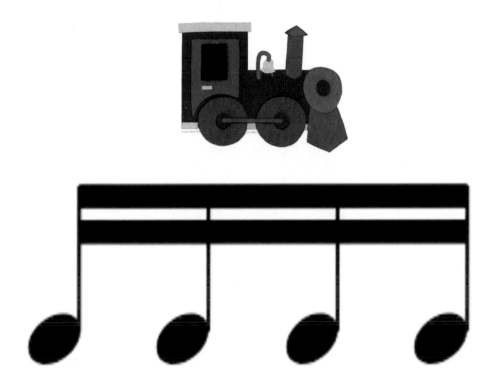

chug-ga

chug-ga

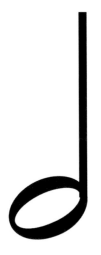 

WEEooo   Stop

1-2

WEEooo   Stop

1-2

beep
beep

bang

beep
beep

bang

beep
beep

stop

beep
beep

bang

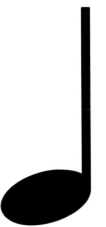

honk   bang

honk   bang

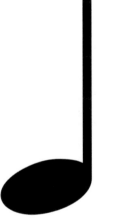

honk

bang

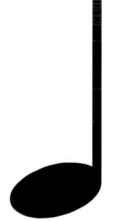

honk   stop

WEEooo

WEEooo

1-2

1-2

WEEooo

WEEooo

1-2

1-2

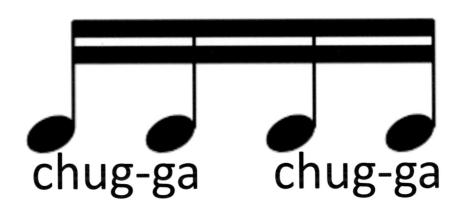

chug-ga   chug-ga

choo   choo

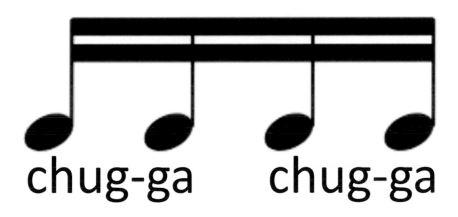

chug-ga   chug-ga

choo   choo

o

SSSShhhhhsssss

1—2—3—4

stop

Make a Color Copy of this page, cut out the pieces so you can play—Beep Beep! On the map pages.

Beep beep! said the little car. Beep Beep! I'm coming down the road. Uh oh! I see a  dump truck unloading some gravel on the side of the road.

Honk! Stop! Phew! Just in time!

Now I hear a firetruck coming my way. Weeooo,  Weeooo. The firetruck is coming closer and closer. Weeooo, Weeooo! I need to pull over for him to get through. He sure is in a hurry. Weeooo! Weeooo!

The firetruck is gone! Now I can go. Beep beep! Beep beep!

Well, well. Here comes the train! I see the steam coming out of the whistle when the engineer has pulled his cord. Toot! Toot! The train is starting to go down the tracks and is coming my way. How I love to see the steam come out. The engine is working hard to get up a head of steam to pull it's load. Chugga chugga. Chugga Chugga. The pressure is building up. The coal and wood are heating up the water to make it heat up. The steam is pushing the piston arms. The engineer releases the pressure into the pistons and it starts turning the wheels and they roll down the track.

Chugga Chugga Chugga Chugga says the train as it goes down the tracks.

Chugga chugga chugga chugga says the train as it turns the corner.

 Here I am at the train crossing as it chugs by. Stop!

Now I can go. Beep Beep! Here is another truck dropping a load of dirt to fill a hole.

Honk! Honk! OK I will be careful and wait. Ok, here I go. Wait! Stop!

I hear a big Bang!

Bang! Bang!

There is a wrecking ball tearing down a building close to my little house. Bang!

Bang! The ball is hitting the building again and again. I sure have had a busy day out

on the road. Glad to be home. Shhhhhhh. I hear the train in the distance,

it is arriving at the station. Time to rest!

I am safe and sound. It has been a big day in the life of a little car. Beep! Beep! I'm

home. Good night.

Bee-eeee-eeep...

The Notes of the scale , their names and how to count them

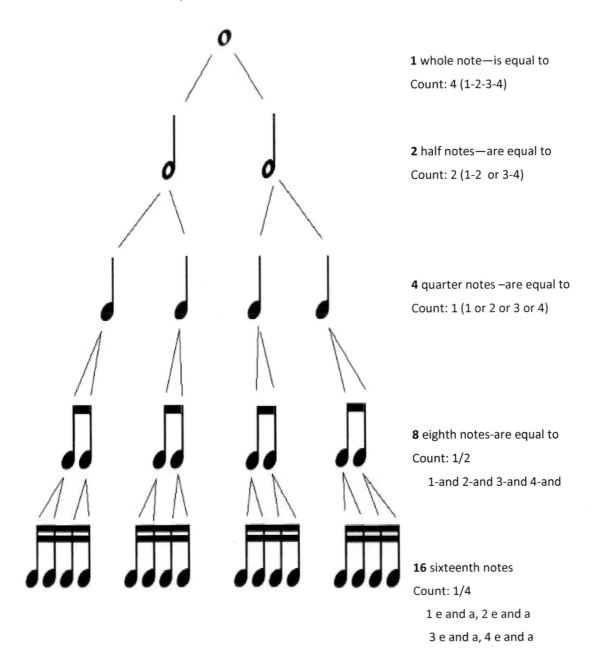

1 whole note—is equal to

Count: 4 (1-2-3-4)

2 half notes—are equal to

Count: 2 (1-2 or 3-4)

4 quarter notes –are equal to

Count: 1 (1 or 2 or 3 or 4)

8 eighth notes-are equal to

Count: 1/2

    1-and 2-and 3-and 4-and

16 sixteenth notes

Count: 1/4

    1 e and a, 2 e and a

    3 e and a, 4 e and a

Made in the USA
Columbia, SC
23 May 2017